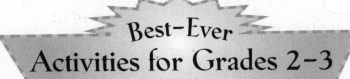

Best-Ever
Activities for Grades 2-3

Addition & Subtraction

Dozens of Activities With Engaging Reproducibles That Kids Will Love...From Creative Teachers Across the Country

BY DEBORAH ROVIN-MURPHY AND FRANK MURPHY

$12 + 3 - 4 + 5 + 67 + 8 + 9 = 100$

SCHOLASTIC
PROFESSIONAL BOOKS

New York • Toronto • London • Auckland • Sydney • Mexico City
New Delhi • Hong Kong • Buenos Aires

For my dad, Abe Rovin, who always showed
a great amount of patience when helping
me with my math homework!
—D.R.M.

For Jim Kinkead—the best math teacher I know!
—F.M.

Thanks a million to all the teachers who submitted ideas:
Peg Arcadi, Cheryll Black, Rita Galloway, Jim Kinkead, Bob Krech, Becky
Mandia, Judy Meagher, Bobbie Williams, and Wendy Wise-Borg.
As always, thanks to Joan Novelli for her expertise and support!

"Using Subtraction" by Lee Blair from ARITHMETIC IN VERSE AND RHYME (Girrard, 1971).

Produced by **Joan Novelli**
Cover and interior design by **Holly Grundon**
Cover and interior art by **Paige Billin-Frye**

ISBN 0-439-29646-3

CONTENTS

CONTENTS

How many legs all together?

About This Book

As teachers of kindergarten through third grade (Debbie) and second through fourth grade (Frank), we see children explore the world of mathematics every day. Children add and subtract coins to pay for lunch, they add and subtract as they share candy or cards, and they add and subtract as they keep score in games. They're immersed in math activities every day without even realizing it!

The activities in this book invite children to take their math explorations further, in ways that are just as appealing as playing a game or sharing a treat. Whether it's a lively game of Musical Math Chairs (see page 10), a math-filled morning message (see page 15), or history-making math stories (see page 35), children will gain confidence in their mathematical abilities and learn important skills as they participate in fun, hands-on activities.

All of the activities support the National Council of Teachers of Mathematics (NCTM) standards for numbers and operations, strengthening skills and concepts in the following areas: understanding numbers, ways of representing numbers, and relationships among numbers; understanding meanings of operations and how they relate to one another; computing fluently and making reasonable estimates; having number sense; estimating a reasonable result for a problem; making sense of numbers, problems, and results; solving problems using relationships among operations; and performing computations in different ways, including mental calculations, estimation, and paper-and-pencil calculations.

Though the activities are organized by addition and subtraction, most of them feature interdisciplinary connections. For example, Math Magic (see page 12) connects social studies and math as children learn about a puzzle that Ben Franklin invented 200 years ago. Math Art (see page 33) encourages art appreciation at the same time it involves children in practicing addition and subtraction skills. Hopscotch Subtraction (see page 24) integrates movement (still important at any age!) with math as children practice counting back. Many of these activities were contributed by teachers from across the country; all of them will enrich your math program and support the math standards in appealing and meaningful ways. Other features of this book include:

- ideas from teachers across the country

- support for the many ways your students learn, including activities that link math with writing, art, music, and movement

- activities that correlate with the NCTM standards

- hands-on science connections

- strategies for second-language learners

- test-taking and assessment tips

- literature-based language arts activities

- interactive displays that encourage children to collaborate in their learning

- computer connections, including software and Web site suggestions

- graphic organizers

- ready-to-use take-home activities

- and many more ideas that will have your students adding and subtracting their way through the day!

Picture the Problem

Tap into visual and spatial learning with an activity that combines fact practice with art.

Cover children's desks or tables with white roll paper. Tape it in place. Give children crayons or markers. Share an addition problem, and invite children to represent it by drawing pictures of their choice. They'll practice addition skills and have some fun drawing at the same time (often a very appealing and stress-free activity for children, which might well lead to better attention and retention of the math they're learning!).

TIP

When children are working with multiple-digit numbers, encourage them to write a regrouped number with a colored marker or write a small addition sign next to the digit to help them remember to add it!

Literature LINK

Anno's Counting Book

by Mitsumasa Anno (HarperCollins, 1986)

This classic, wordless picture book is perfect for introducing counting. While the pictures seem simple at first, with each turn of the page the counting becomes more complicated. Starting with zero and working up to twelve, there are so many things to see on each page. Children will love finding and counting various things on each page that correspond to each number. An explanation at the back of the book offers a history of numbers.

Button Count

Before children can add multiple-digit numbers that require trading, they must understand the concept of trading 10 ones for 1 ten. Try this fun activity to reinforce this concept.

- Give each child a small paper cup of buttons. Have children take out one button for each button on their clothing that day.

- Assign partners to children. Have partners combine their buttons and then use manipulatives (such as "tens sticks" and "ones cubes") to represent their buttons in tens and ones.

- Bring students together to repeat the activity on a larger scale. Have children keep their tens bundles but pool their ones to see how many more tens they can make. Have them trade each group of 10 ones cubes for a tens stick. Count by tens together to see how many buttons the class is wearing!

To assess children's understanding of ones and tens, invite them to draw seven blocks, then draw eight blocks. Have them ring a group of ten to show how to group tens and ones.

Twenty Wins

Invite students to practice adding four digits (and squeeze some subtraction in, too) with this challenging two-player game.

- Make copies of the reproducible grid on page 36. Give one to each child.

- Have children play in pairs, taking turns rolling two number cubes. Players can choose to add or subtract the two numbers on the cubes, then write the sum or difference in any box on the grid.

- A player scores a point when he or she can successfully put four digits together into a square (four boxes that form a square) to total 20. Students can use a highlighter or crayon to mark successful squares on the grid. The game continues until one player has received a given number of points or until the board is full of numbers.

Wendy Wise-Borg
Rider University
Lawrenceville, New Jersey

House of Addition

Invite your students to build a fun-filled house of addition and open lots of doors (and windows) to fun math-fact practice.

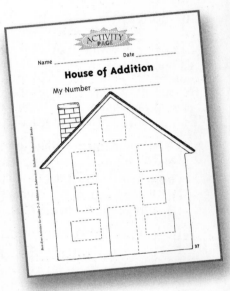

Give each child a copy of the house template on page 37. Have students fill in a number (at the top) and write different numbers on the window flaps and front door. The number at the top will be the missing addend for the numbers on the house (each combination, then, making a number sentence). Have students cut the windows and door into movable flaps and then glue the house to a sheet of construction paper, placing glue around the edges but not behind the movable flaps. Have students write the sum of each problem behind each flap. Display the houses of addition (flaps closed) and let students practice their math facts by solving the problems on each house and lifting the flaps to check their answers.

Bobbie Williams
Brookwood Elementary
Snellville, Georgia

TIP

For a challenge, have students select the number that will serve as the missing addend and record it on the back of the paper, not in the space provided. When you display the houses, children will have to determine the missing addend by looking at the numbers on the windows and door and the answer behind each flap.

Literature LINK

Domino Addition

by Lynette Long (Charlesbridge, 1996)

This colorful picture book uses dominoes to teach the concept of addition. Sets of dominoes on each colorful page represent sums from zero to twelve. Students can strengthen their skills by adding them up. After sharing the book, invite children to use real dominoes to create and practice addition number sentences.

Roll the Number Cubes

Invite pairs of children to play this quick and easy game together to create and complete two-digit addition problems.

You'll need two number cubes (preferably one cube with the numbers 1 to 6 and another with the numbers 4 to 9), a pencil, and paper. One child rolls the cubes and the partner writes a two-digit number from the cubes. So, for example, if a child rolls a 1 and a 3, the other child could write 31. The first child rolls again, creating a second number that the partner writes underneath. The partner completes the addition and the first child checks the work. Children switch places and play again.

Counting on Buildings

Invite children to build structures out of ones cubes and tens blocks (and hundreds blocks if available)—and build mental math skills, too.

Encourage children to count up the value of the cubes and blocks as they use them and to record the "sum" of their structure. Providing children with free time to explore building with these blocks will help them gain familiarity with the amounts. As a challenge, invite children to determine the sum of the cubes and blocks before they build. Have them record this number on a slip of paper. Classmates can estimate the sum represented in the structures, then see how close they came.

Literature
LINK

The Grapes of Math
by Greg Tang (Scholastic Press, 2001)

This award-winning picture book uses brightly colored illustrations to introduce creative techniques for solving math problems. Described as "mind-stretching math riddles," the text is written in verse and will help children look at math in completely new ways.

Musical Math Chairs

Incorporate movement, music, and math with this skill-strengthening activity. You'll need a radio (or tape or CD player and music).

On each child's desk, place a pencil and a sheet of addition problems. Use various worksheets to provide experience with different kinds of problems. For example, at one child's desk, place a sheet of word problems. At another desk, place a sheet of one-digit addition problems (for example, 3 + 5 = __). You can also provide activity sheets for two-digit addition problems, problems that invite kids to find the missing addend, and so on. Tell students that they're going to help one another solve all of the problems on their sheets. Then start the music and have students get up and walk (or dance!) around the room while the music is playing. Stop the music and have students sit in the closest seat. Have each child solve a problem on the paper at that seat, then start the music again and repeat the activity. Continue until all papers have been completed! In the process, each child will have had practice trying different kinds of problems.

Stick to It!

Every classroom can always use new math manipulatives. Invite students to make these artistic manipulatives while learning about tens and ones.

- Give children glue, craft sticks, and various trinkets, such as plastic beads, dried beans, and stickers.
- Have children arrange the objects on the sticks in tens and glue them in place. Children can sign their names to the backs of the sticks with phrases such as "Created by Diego" or "Built by Amy." Let the sticks dry, and use them for future math activities. For example, have students line up the craft sticks on a chalkboard tray one at a time and count by tens. How many objects all together? Can they represent this in a number sentence? Go further and use the sticks to introduce multiplication (10 x [the number of students] = [the total number of objects]).

When learning about regrouping with addition, allow students to use a highlighter to mark the ones column before they solve a problem. This will visually remind them to begin with the ones column and to move the regrouped number they just added into the tens column.

Sum Stories

One of the NCTM standards is the ability to communicate mathematically. Here's an interactive display that can help students meet this standard.

- ๑ Display a white board and above it write the title "Sum Stories." Add a decorative border and write a number sentence at the top.

- ๑ Invite a child (or two children) to write an addition story about the number sentence. Children can draw pictures to go with the story, then leave it on display for the day to share with classmates.

- ๑ Each day, erase the board, change the number sentence, and let new children write and illustrate a story.

Judy Meagher
Student Teacher Supervisor
Bozeman, Montana

Using Braille flash cards is a great way to incorporate kinesthetic learning for all children. Check these Web sites for these materials and more: Creative Adaptations for Learning **www.cals.org** and **www.uncl goose.com**.

SECOND Language LEARNERS

To help second-language learners better understand the addition and subtraction skills you're teaching, invite several children to act out a word problem that a child has written. The entire class will enjoy the acting experience, and second-language learners will be able to understand the math in new ways.

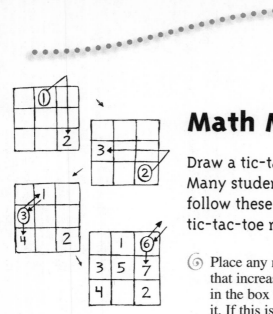

Math Magic

Draw a tic-tac-toe grid on the board. Ask students what it is. Many students will recognize the familiar gameboard. Then follow these directions to amaze your students with a little tic-tac-toe math magic! (See sample magic square, left.)

- Place any number in the center box of the top row. Using numbers that increase or decrease consecutively, place each remaining number in the box that is one higher and directly to the right of the one before it. If this is not possible, use one of the following alternatives:

  If the next move is on top of the square, go to the bottom of that column and write the number in that box.

  If the next move is to the right of the square, go to the far left of that row and write the number in that box.

  If the next move is in a box that already has a number or is on top of and to the right of the whole square, go to the box directly below the previous one and write the number in that box.

- Ask students if they notice anything about the numbers in the squares. List all responses, then draw another tic-tac-toe grid on the board.

- Now, share *Ben Franklin and the Magic Squares*. (See below.) When you get to the section about Ben Franklin creating the magic square, use the blank tic-tac-toe grid on the board to model the placement of the numbers. Review the addition inside the square, across, down, and diagonally. Then give children copies of the reproducible tic-tac-toe grid on page 38 and invite them to create their own magic squares.

Challenge students with a "problem of the day" that consists of a magic square with a few missing numbers. Students have to find the magic sum, then find missing addends to complete the square—great practice for using multiple strategies and adding with three digits.

Literature LINK

Ben Franklin and the Magic Squares

by Frank Murphy (Random House, 2001)

This easy reader combines history and math and serves as a great springboard for creating really interesting math puzzles. It is a true story about Ben Franklin and how he made the math puzzles called magic squares.

Magic Triangles

Ben Franklin's squares aren't the only shapes that can be magical. Invite your students to pair up and have fun strengthening addition skills with this challenging problem.

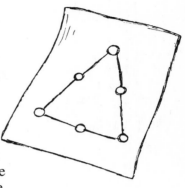

Draw a triangle on the chalkboard. Draw a circle at each angle and in the middle of each line. (See sample.) Note that the lines do not pass through the circles. Have students copy the triangle on paper or mini-chalkboards. Then challenge them to arrange the numbers 1, 2, 3, 4, 5, and 6 in the circles so that the sum of each side of the triangle is the same. After children complete the triangle, compare answers to see if they are correct and to see if there is more than one possible arrangement. Ask children to think about what would happen if each digit were increased by 10, 100, or 1,000. Make new magic triangles and try it out!

Peg Arcadi
Homeschool Teacher
Trumansburg, New York

The Greatest Sum Game

Invite students to improve their number sense and addition skills with a game that challenges players to make an addition problem with the greatest sum.

⊚ Have children pair up to play. Give each player a copy of the game board on page 39.

⊚ Each pair of children will need a set of the digit cards on page 40. Have students cut out the digit cards, shuffle them, and place them facedown between players.

⊚ Players take turns taking a card and writing that number in any box. Players continue taking turns until all boxes have been filled.

⊚ Now each player adds the numbers in each set of squares to complete the addition problem. Have players circle their greatest sum and then exchange papers to check each other's addition. Players then compare their answers. The player with the greatest sum wins.

TIP

Change the game to make an addition problem with the smallest sum. Further challenge students by making the object of the game to have a sum come closest to a certain number without going over.

Math Connections
Word Wall

Help your students make math connections in the world around them by building an illustrated word wall.

Invite children to think of ways to represent ten or one hundred. Encourage them to be creative—for example, decade, dime, ten dollar bill, ten-yard line, ten pennies, and the Roman numeral X (for example, on an old building or in the page numbers of a book) all represent ten. Century, hundred dollar bill, Sacagawea coin, the Roman numeral C, and a football field all represent one hundred. Write ideas on sentence strips and display to make a word wall. To reinforce the concept of ten and one hundred in the real world, have children draw and display pictures to illustrate the words.

Literature
LINK

Counting on Frank

by Rod Clement (Gareth Stevens, 1991)

In this wild story, a young boy and his dog, Frank, examine everything from peas to ballpoint pens, experiencing all kinds of counting fun. The boy's imagination allows readers to learn challenging ways to calculate some weird things. A guide in the back gives hints and answers to problems.

TIP

Remind students about the importance of aligning multiple-digit numbers when adding and regrouping. Give students problems written horizontally on chart paper or a blackboard. Invite students to write down the problems on grid paper or lined paper turned sideways. Using these papers will help students position the numbers in the correct place-value column.

Morning Message Math

Use your morning message as a way to reinforce addition and subtraction skills every day. Here are a few ideas to try:

- Ask students to see if the day's date is the sum of a double—for example, if the date is the 24th, this is the sum of a double (12 + 12).

- Invite students to write an addition or subtraction sentence that has the day's date as the answer.

- Let students count the number of words in the morning message by twos.

- Incorporate a sentence in your morning message that asks students to add or subtract to find an answer—for example, "Monday it was 73°. Tuesday it was 84°. Which day was warmer? By how much? How hot do you think it will be today?" Students can record answers beneath the morning message.

Visit an outstanding math Web site (for kids and teachers) packed with games, activities, and more at **www.cool math4kids.com**.

Nine Digits Equal One Hundred

Challenge students to add numbers to make 100 with this mind-bending activity.

Write the sequence of digits 1–9 on the board. Ask children to copy the digits, leaving a space between each digit. Invite children to place plus or minus signs between some spaces so that the answer to the number sentence will be 100. (Remind them that the numbers have to stay in the same sequence.) Some possible solutions are:

$$1 + 2 + 3 - 4 + 5 + 6 + 78 + 9 = 100$$
$$12 - 3 - 4 + 5 - 6 + 7 + 89 = 100$$
$$123 + 4 - 5 + 67 - 89 = 100$$

$$12 + 3 - 4 + 5 + 67 + 8 + 9 = 100$$

Bob Krech
Dutch Neck Elementary
Princeton, New Jersey

Count On to Win

Invite children to practice the skill of "counting on" with number and dot cubes.

Provide a number cube (1–6) and a dot cube (1–6). Let pairs of students take turns rolling both cubes. When a player rolls a 1, 2, or 3 on the dot cube, the player says the number on the number cube, then counts on the number of dots to find the sum. Players can keep a tally of how many times they got to "count on" (how many times the dot cube landed on 1, 2, or 3). The player who gets to count on the most times wins.

Literature LINK

Mission Addition

by Loreen Leedy (Holiday House, 1997)

This picture book is presented in the form of comic strips. Hippo teacher Miss Prime and her students practice all kinds of addition concepts while solving various problems that have them adding columns of numbers, creating addition sentences, and adding dollar amounts.

SECOND Language LEARNERS

The concept of counting on will be unfamiliar to most second-language learners. Explain that to count on means to start with a certain number and count by ones to add. (Usually children are taught to use this strategy when adding 0, 1, 2, or 3.) Ask children to think of other ways they have heard the word *on* used—for example: "The sock is on my foot" or "Turn on the lights." List these examples on the board. Invite students to draw and color pictures showing different meanings of the word *on*, including the phrase *count on* in math.

___ Ways to Get to 11 Class Book

To reinforce different ways to make a sum, make a class book modeled on the story *12 Ways to Get to 11*. (See below.)

- Take time to review the story. Which was your students' favorite way of adding up to 11? Which was the most unusual? The funniest?

- Ask children to suggest other ways to get to 11. Then give each child a sheet of drawing paper. Have children make up and illustrate a new way to get to 11.

- Put the pages together to create a class book. Add a cover with the title "___ Ways to Get to 11."

- Fill in the blank with the number of kids in your classroom, then bind the pages and let children take turns reading aloud their pages and sharing their illustrations.

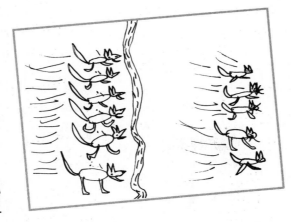

Literature LINK

12 Ways to Get to 11

by Eve Merriam (Simon & Schuster, 1993)

"One, two, three, four, five, six, seven, eight, nine, ten...twelve. Where's eleven?" This question starts the quest for different ways to add up to eleven. From counting six peanuts and five pieces of popcorn at the circus to counting a sow and ten baby piglets, children have the opportunity to investigate colorful illustrations while learning about different ways to make a sum.

For a Web site full of great addition and subtraction games, go to Mrs. Dowling's Fun and Games Page: **www.dowlin central.com/ MrsD/fun.html.**

Teach the following strategies to make number operations easier: doubles (such as 4 + 4 = 8), doubles plus 1 (such as 4 + 5 = 9), fact families (such as 2 + 3 = 5, 3 + 2 = 5, 5 – 2 = 3, 5 – 3 = 2), turn-around facts (such as 7 + 3 = 10 and 3 + 7 = 10), counting up (adding 1, 2, or 3 to a larger number), and counting back (subtracting 1, 2, or 3 from a larger number).

Reflecting Doubles

Invite your students to visually enhance their understanding of doubles by using a mirror. The effect is magical, and students will want to do it again and again.

🌀 Give students different amounts of small items like candies, buttons, or jacks. Have students place them on their desks. Ask students if they can think of a way to double the amount of items on their desks without getting any more.

🌀 Hand out small mirrors. Ask students to predict what will happen when they hold the mirror right up against the items. Let students try it out and then count the items they see.

🌀 Have them write number sentences to show the "doubles" math, then try magically doubling other items on their desks.

Literature LINK

Two of Everything
by Lily Toy Hong (Whitman, 1993)

In this Chinese folktale, an old couple finds a magic pot that doubles everything that is put into it. The trouble starts when the old wife falls into the pot! After sharing the book, reinforce the concept of adding doubles by bringing in a large, black plastic cauldron. Fill the cauldron with everyday items. Prepare to amaze the kids by secretly placing a set number of items in the cauldron and then handing out the matching number of items to students. Ask students to place their items in the cauldron. Then magically pull out the item—now doubled!

Mail Math

Students practice real-life math skills while combining different numbers to create a set amount of money.

TIP

- Make copies of the reproducible stamps on page 41. Distribute blank envelopes along with a set of stamps to each student.

- Have students write their own names and addresses on the envelope, and explain that letters weighing more than a certain amount require different amounts of postage.

- Select one student to be Postmaster General. Have that student stand in the front of the room and announce the amount of postage needed to mail their letters.

- After calling out the amount, have students combine stamps on the envelope to make exactly the amount they need. Let students share the different combinations they used. Record them on the chalkboard, along with the total. Then select another student to be the Postmaster General and give a different total to try.

Use everyday classroom procedures to observe students' proficiency with addition and subtraction. Lunch count, attendance, paper passing, and other routines all lend themselves to real word-problem solving.

SECOND Language LEARNERS

Picture clues are a great way to have your second-language learners make connections between the concrete action and abstract vocabulary and symbols used to solve problems. Post pictures of a set with an action. (For example, display 5 candy bar wrappers and put an X through 3.) Underneath the pictures, write the subtraction sentence in both symbols and words—for example, 5 - 3 = _____ and "I had five candy bars and ate three. How many do I have left?"

Take a Turn

Children love playing games. Capitalize on this interest by using familiar games to practice math facts.

First, choose games that require players to pick a card in order to go forward. (Chutes and Ladders and Candy Land are good examples.) Substitute math fact flash cards (your students can make them on index cards) for the original game cards. Students need to give the correct answer to the math fact problem to find out how many spaces to move forward. This is an easy way for teachers to create games for centers as well as a useful way to recycle old game boards.

Wendy Wise-Borg
Rider University
Lawrenceville, New Jersey

Calendar Subtraction

Have some fun figuring out how many school days there are each month and strengthen subtraction skills at the same time.

⚙ Begin by inviting students to suggest ways they could find out how many school days there are this month—for example, they could count up all the weekdays and subtract the number of school holidays that fall during the week or subtract the number of weekend days and holidays from the total number of days in the month.

⚙ Try out one of the methods together and write the resulting number sentence and answer on a sentence strip.

⚙ Have students work together to write a few sentences to go with the number sentence, explaining what it shows. Display both next to the calendar. As you repeat this activity each month, have children make comparisons: "Which month has had the most school days so far? the fewest?"

Towering Comparisons

Children love to compare sizes of the world's tallest structures. Strengthen their ability to find differences by supplying them with data to compare.

Display information about the Statue of Liberty, Washington Monument, and Mount Rushmore or the Empire State Building, Sears Tower, and Petronas Tower. (See How High, right, for data.) Have children use the data to calculate the differences between the height of the various structures. Use the activity to highlight the importance of recognizing that subtraction does not always mean taking away—it can mean comparing. To go further, let students research other tall structures to compare. Invite them to illustrate their results and display them on a bulletin board or in the pages of a class book.

Peg Arcadi
Homeschool Teacher
Trumansburg, New York

Race to Zero

Students will have fun playing this backward game while reinforcing and practicing their subtraction skills.

Divide the class into groups of two to three students. Each group will need a copy of the game board on page 42, a number cube, and a marker for each player. Have players put their markers on the space marked 30. Players take turns rolling the number cube and subtracting that number from their position on the game board. The first player to get to zero wins the game!

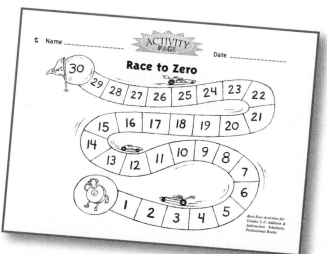

How High?

Petronas Tower:
1,476 feet

Sears Tower:
1,454 feet

Empire State Building:
1,250 feet

Mount Rushmore:
5,725 feet

Washington Monument:
555 feet

Statue of Liberty:
151 feet
(base to torch)

305 feet
(base of pedestal to torch)

Make paper, pencils, and calculators available to check each player's accuracy.

Math Snack

Students will enjoy math even more when they know they can eat the problems when they are done! Plan a math snack picnic to reinforce combining different-sized sets.

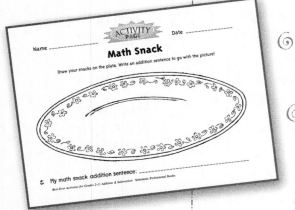

- Invite families to send in snack foods to share. Items that come in small pieces work well—for example, pretzels, carrot sticks, crackers, and grapes.

- Arrange the snacks on a table, along with plates, eating utensils (if necessary), and napkins. Have students select foods they'd like for snack and place them on the plate.

- Before they take their first bite, give each child a copy of page 43. Have children draw pictures of their snacks and then write addition sentences to go with them—for example, "5 carrots + 12 grapes + 3 crackers = 20 snacks)."

- Strengthen subtraction skills by telling students to eat their snacks! Have them pause periodically to share math sentences with one another about what they're eating and what's left—for example, "five carrots take away one carrot equals four carrot sticks."

Peg Arcadi
Homeschool Teacher
Trumansburg, New York

Check for food allergies before serving snacks.

Literature LINK

The Candy Counting Book: Delicious Ways to Add and Subtract

by Lisa McCourt (Bridgewater, 1999)

This colorful picture book uses all kinds of classic candies and delicious story problems to help kids learn about addition and subtraction. Let your students think of their own delicious ways to add and subtract. Use them to make a mouth-watering display!

Subtraction Action Word Wall

Strengthen students' understanding of subtraction and the language involved by sharing real-life subtraction situations and using them to build a word wall.

- Read the following situation to children (or make up your own using students' names): "John had 24 sheets of paper. He gave 12 sheets to Nico. How many sheets of paper did John have left?"

- Ask children to discuss the actions involved in these situations. (*giving away* and *comparing*) Ask: "Which words show the subtraction action?" (*gave* and *have left*)

- Repeat the activity with new situations. Incorporate subtraction words such as *have left* and *how many more than* to show the different operations in the subtraction problems.

- Follow up by asking students to volunteer additional "action" words for subtraction problems—for example, how many more, how many less, greater than, less than, have left, have now, and have before. List students' responses on sentence strips or posterboard to make a Subtraction Action Word Wall.

Subtraction Straws

Students break apart bundles of straws to make the function of regrouping more visual and hands-on.

Divide the class into small groups. Give each group a handful of straws and some trash bag ties. Have children use the ties to bundle straws in groups of ten. Ask them to leave at least nine straws unbundled. When students are ready, give each group a subtraction problem to solve. Have students match the number of straws with the problem and decide whether or not they'll need to untie and break apart a tens bundle. So, to show 12 - 9, students would start with a bundle of ten straws plus two single straws, then break apart the tens bundle to subtract nine.

Many children say "take away" for subtraction signs—for example, "four take away two." Remind them that subtraction also includes comparing numbers—for example, comparing children's height at the beginning and end of the year to see how much they've grown.

Hopscotch Subtraction

Take subtraction out to the playground by playing this variation of hopscotch.

Draw a hopscotch lane, or use the ones already painted on your playground. Make a giant number cube by covering a square-shaped tissue box with construction paper and writing the numbers 1 to 6 on it. Let students take turns rolling the number cube and, starting at 10, hopping back (subtracting) the number that appears on the cube. The goal is to hop back (in as many turns as it takes) until they reach 1 exactly. Players skip turns if they roll a number that would result in going beyond the 1 on the hopscotch lane.

Subtraction Poetry

Get your students excited about subtraction with writing and poetry!

Give each child a copy of the poem "Using Subtraction" on page 44. Read the poem aloud, and invite students to fill in the blanks with things they would like to see subtracted from their world—for example, they might fill in such pesky problems as homework or rainy days, or they might suggest more serious concerns, such as poverty or pollution. Invite students to brainstorm more ideas, and have them fill the blanks with as many things they wish they could subtract.

Literature LINK

Subtraction Action
by Loreen Leedy (Holiday House, 2000)

A hippo teacher named Miss Prime and her class learn about subtraction at the school fair. From cookies disappearing in a puppet show to prices being reduced at refreshment stands, this picture book is a great springboard for introducing subtraction concepts. Colorful illustrations provide visual clues to help with the problems.

The Greatest Difference Game

This game reinforces number sense and gives children practice subtracting three-digit numbers. You can adapt it to use with more or fewer digits.

- You'll need three number cubes and each child will need paper and pencil. (The game will work best with cubes that have the digits 0–5, 2–7, and 4–9.) Students can play in pairs or more.

- A player rolls three number cubes. Both (or all) players use the three digits to write a three-digit number. Each player should hide the number he or she writes.

- Another player rolls the cubes again. Both (or all) players make another three-digit number and write it down. Each player then subtracts the lesser number from the greater number. Each player's difference is the score he or she uses for that round.

- Players continue taking turns and recording each three-digit number and score for the round on a sheet of paper. The first player to reach a specified number (1,000 is a good start) is the winner. After playing, invite children to discuss any strategies they used. For example, ask students why and when they may have written the highest or lowest number possible.

Jim Kinkead
Newtown Elementary
Newtown, Pennsylvania

Make a Math Alien

Your students will use their imagination while practicing out-of-this-world addition and subtraction facts.

Give each child a copy of page 45. Have students fill in the blanks without solving the equations—for example, "5 + 2 = _____ eyes." Let children exchange papers to solve each other's equations, then use the answers (*7 eyes, 11 heads,* and so on) as directions to create math aliens. When children have finished creating the aliens, have them share their out-of-this-world art with the classmate they traded papers with.

Make extra copies of the Make a Math Alien activity sheet and complete them with problems you want children to solve. Place the papers at a math center and let children create more creatures while strengthening their addition and subtraction skills.

Problem-Solving Stories

Integrate language arts with mathematical problem-solving by having students write literature-inspired word problems.

Invite students to think of a character and event from a favorite book. Model for students how to turn both into a word problem—for example, "Curious George has to gather 12 bananas for the man in the yellow hat. He already has 3. How many more does he need?" Have students write and illustrate a word problem that features their character and event. Students can place their stories in the matching books for other students to solve.

School-Days Subtraction

Get your students excited about summer, whether it's late or early in the year!

Tell students how many school days there are in the school year and display this information near the classroom calendar. Ask students how many days they've been in school. They can use a school calendar to find out. Now invite them to use their three-digit subtraction skills to find out how many school days are left in the school year. Keep a running count each day or each week and post it alongside the calendar.

Literature LINK

Shark Swimathon: Subtracting Two-Digit Numbers

by Stuart J. Murphy (HarperCollins, 2001)

A shark swim team practices two-digit subtraction while trying to reach a goal of 75 laps. The subtraction gets more difficult as the story progresses, and a swim team coach is on hand to explain the process in each example. Perceptive children will note that the swimmers' performance improves with practice!

TIP

For fast-paced flashcard practice in a game format, try School Zone's *Interactive Flash Action*, a software program for grades 1–4. Players solve problems while competing against a clock or against another player. Players can customize games to a specific number family from 0–12.

Choral Countdown

Many students use the skill of counting back and make the mistake of starting with the number that will be decreased. Strengthen your students' skills in counting back by regularly doing this choral countdown.

- Before you begin a choral countdown, give students some practice in starting with the correct number. Say a number, and have students call out the number that is one less than that number. Repeat this quite a few times to make sure students understand the concept. Then try a choral countdown.

- Announce a number and tell students what number you want them to count back to. On your cue, have students start counting back together. To keep track of how many numbers they're subtracting, have them make tally marks on dry erase boards or mini-chalkboards.

- After arriving at the target number, they can add up the tally marks to determine the number they subtracted from the original number.

TIP

Challenge children by setting the number to be subtracted or the amount to be counted back (such as 9 or 10). Say the starting number. Have students then call out the number that is one less and continue counting back. What number will students count back to?

SECOND Language LEARNERS

Using a large calendar to practice counting back makes the activity more visual for second-language learners. Point to the numbers on the calendar as students count them back aloud. Seeing the numbers will give students another way to remember the words and will build not only number sense but vocabulary, too.

Round and Round Comparisons

In this activity, students move to music and get lots of practice with subtraction skills in the process.

⟲ Divide the class into two equal groups. Distribute Unifix cubes or other manipulatives to each student. Vary the number of manipulatives you give each child (for example, from 1 to 20). Have one of the groups form a circle. Have the other group form a larger circle around the first group.

⟲ Play music and have children move around in their circles. Both circles can go in the same direction, or you can have the circles move in opposite directions. When you stop the music, have each student in the outer circle partner up with the student across from him or her in the inner circle.

⟲ Have outer/inner circle partners match up their Unifix cubes and use subtraction to compare who has more and who has less. After students have made their comparisons, put on the music and play again.

It's in the Bag

Students use critical thinking and practice finding missing addends while figuring out the number of hidden objects in a bag.

⟲ Distribute manipulatives and a paper bag to pairs of students. The manipulatives can match a theme students are studying— for example, if the theme is explorers, you might use gold coins. If you're exploring oceans, you might use fish-shaped crackers. To connect with a unit on bugs, use plastic insects.

⟲ Have one student (A) in each pair set out a certain number of manipulatives for the other child (B) to see and count. The remaining manipulatives should be placed to the side.

⟲ Have partner B close his or her eyes while partner A puts some of the manipulatives in the bag. Partner B then has to guess how many objects are in the bag by counting the number of objects that are out of the bag and using addition or subtraction to figure out the missing addend. Have partners switch places and play again.

Strengthen students' skills with *Mega Math Blaster* (Davidson), a software program packed with arcade-style games that reinforce relationships among numbers and meanings of operations and build fluency in computing.

Who Am I? Math Riddles

Do your students love to create riddles? Invite children to choose a favorite number to create lift-the-flap subtraction math riddles for a friend.

Make copies of the reproducible Who Am I? riddle sheet on page 46. Have students cut out a square of construction paper to fit over the answer space. They can make a flap to hide their answers by gluing the top edge of the construction paper square to the top edge of the answer space. Have children complete the riddle for any number they like and then lift the flap and write the answer in the space provided. Display the riddles on a bulletin board or in the hallway and invite classmates or other children in the school to solve the riddles and lift the flaps to check their answers.

First off the Bridge

Students can practice counting on and counting back as they try to be the first person off the bridge in this game.

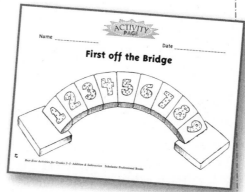

Have students pick partners. Give each pair of students a game board (see page 47), eight index cards labeled "ADD 1," "ADD 2," "ADD 3," "ADD 0," "SUBTRACT 1," "SUBTRACT 2," "SUBTRACT 3," and "SUBTRACT 0," and two game markers (such as dried beans). Have students place their markers in the middle of the bridge and the cards facedown in a pile. To play, children take turns choosing a card from the pile and either adding (going forward) or subtracting (going backward) from their position on the bridge. The goal is to be the first person who gets off the bridge. Players do not have to land exactly on the first stone off the bridge to win. The player can end up multiple steps off to win.

Becky Mandia
Newtown Elementary
Newtown, Pennsylvania

Place additional copies of the First off the Bridge game, along with simple directions, in resealable plastic bags. Let children take turns borrowing the games to play with their families. Include a response sheet in the math packs so that families can share comments and strategies.

All Through the Year

At the start of a new month, invite children to combine math and science to learn more about the weather.

- ⑤ Set up a schedule to have children observe the weather each day.

- ⑤ Make a chart to record whether the day was sunny, snowy, cloudy, rainy, or snowy.

- ⑤ Have children use tally marks to record the information on the chart. They can also use words or pictures to record the same information each day on the calendar. At the end of the month, have children work in groups to discover differences between sunny days and rainy days, cloudy days and sunny days, and so on. Remind children to add the tally marks first, then subtract the numbers to find differences. Discuss the findings, and post them next to the calendar.

TiP

Mix up the puppets and place them at a center. Let students work with partners to reorganize the families and put on mini puppet shows that incorporate the math.

Art

Fact Family Puppets

Help children understand relationships between addition and subtraction by creating a puppet "family of facts."

- ⑤ Invite students to write a simple math equation on a sheet of paper. Explain that each of their math equations is part of a fact family. Each member of this family has the same three numbers—for example, $2 + 3 = 5$, $3 + 2 = 5$, $5 - 2 = 3$, $5 - 3 = 2$. Have students write down the rest of the members of their fact families on the sheet of paper.

- ⑤ Give each child four large craft sticks. Have students use a marker to write each of the fact family member equations at the bottom of a craft stick.

- ⑤ Now for the fun part. Give children various craft supplies, such as yarn, glitter, felt, stickers, and colored stones. Let children use the materials to create each "family member." When they're finished, let students introduce their family to the class.

Fact Family Jumping

This lively game reinforces relationships among numbers and helps children learn their math facts!

⊚ Write the digits from an addition or subtraction sentence on paper plates. For example, write the numbers 3, 4, and 7 on three plates (one number per plate). Place the plates on the floor (numbers facing up) to form a triangle.

⊚ Model fact family jumping with addition by asking a student to stand on the 3. Have the student shout "Three" and then jump from the 3 to the 4. The student then shouts "plus four" and then jumps to the 7. The student shouts "equals seven" and then hops off.

⊚ Try the same thing in reverse to model subtraction. Have the child start on 7 and then jump to either 3 or 4, then to the remaining plate for the answer.

⊚ Let children make their own fact-family jumping games. (Check to make sure they're each doing a different one.) Let students rotate to one another's games to "jump" the fact families.

⊚ Make this activity more challenging by turning over a plate and hiding a number. The student will have to shout out the missing number.

Add or Subtract? Morning Message

Strengthen students' critical-thinking skills with a morning message that combines addition and subtraction.

Display a certain number of manipulatives (magnets, stickers, and markers) by your morning message. Clip a number card to the message (for example, the number 14 written on an index card). In your message, invite students to count how many manipulatives there are (for example, 10) and write it in their notebooks. Ask them to decide whether they need to add or subtract manipulatives to get to the number on the card (for example, 10 + or − __ = 14). Have students write the problems in their notebooks. Let them share their answers and strategies at your morning meeting or math time. Let children demonstrate with the manipulatives what they did to solve the problem.

Rita Galloway
Bonham Elementary
Harlingen, Texas

Hop to It

Students actively solve addition and subtraction problems as they hop up and down a giant number line.

◉ Make a number line by taping a ten-foot piece of masking tape on the floor. Tape number cards (1–20) at 6-inch intervals along the number line.

◉ Write addition or subtraction problems on sentence strips, and you're ready to play! To play with the class, line up students and hold the number sentences facedown. Flash a sentence strip to the first student. Have this child hop out the problem on the number line to land on the answer. Remind students to always stand on the higher number first before jumping forward—for example, if the problem is 5 + 3, the student stands on the number 5 and hops three spaces forward to find out that the answer is 8.

◉ Encourage students to count on or count back out loud as they hop up or down the number line to the answer. A fun variation of this activity is to give the students two numbers (for example, 3 and 9) and ask them how many hops it takes to get from one to the other.

Cheryll Black
Newtown Elementary
Newtown, Pennsylvania

Laminate number line strips on each student's desk. Students can use these number lines as "helpers" to count on, count back, and skip-count.

Add/Subtract Graphic Organizer

This interactive bulletin board lets students access the correct terms when discussing math.

Ask students to name words or phrases that relate to addition and subtraction—for example, *equals, addend, difference*. List each word or phrase on a separate index card. Create a large Venn diagram on a bulletin board. Label one side "Addition" and the other "Subtraction." Let children take turns selecting a card and leading a discussion about where the card belongs. Have them place the cards in the correct section, either in the addition or subtraction section or in the overlapping section to show that it goes with both. As you continue to study addition and subtraction, add new cards. Students can use the board as a vocabulary reference when they're writing about or discussing the two operations.

Jim Kinkead
Newtown Elementary
Newtown, Pennsylvania

Math Art

Math is everywhere! Invite students to explore math in their world by creating math problems to match a picture or drawing.

◎ Gather assorted art prints, books with lots of art, pictures from calendars, and so on. Display them in a central location for students to browse.

◎ Ask each child to choose a piece of art to explore. After giving children time to look closely at their work of art, challenge them to create word problems for mathematical equations that match the art. For example, a math sentence to go with Vincent van Gogh's *In the Bedroom* is: "How many chairs? How many chair legs all together?"

◎ Use students' word problems and the artwork to create a display. Take time to solve the problems as a class.

◎ Encourage children to revisit the display on their own for more practice. Children will enjoy adding to the display with new math art.

How many legs all together?

Literature LINK

A Child's Book of Art

by Lucy Micklethwait (Dorling Kindersley, 1993)

This oversized book features paintings and prints that encourage art appreciation while introducing math concepts, too, including numbers and shapes. It's a perfect resource for Math Art (see above), and includes works by Cassat, van Gogh, Matisse, Degas, Hiroshige, Suiseki, Renoir, Rivera, and others.

Around the World With Numbers

Enrich children's understanding of numbers and world languages by letting them create word problems using words or symbols for numbers in another language.

After sharing *Count Your Way Through China* (see below), and other books in the series, let children work together to make a word wall or poster listing the number names for 1–10 in each country's native language. Let children choose a favorite language and write a number sentence using the number words in that language. Have students arrange their word problems on a display. Add maps and flags to complete the display.

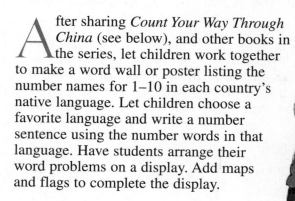

For a Web site with a big listing of picture books with math connections, go to **cehd.ewu. edu/cehd/ faculty/ntodd/4 50Rebekah.html**.

Literature LINK

Count Your Way Through China

by Jim Haskins (Carolrhoda, 1988)

Share this informative story to explore China and learn to count to ten in another language. Other books in the series introduce counting to ten in French, Spanish, Italian, and other languages. Use the information to create a picture word wall or display that shows how to count to ten in each language. For a related activity, see Around the World With Numbers, above.

Take-Home Activity:
Math Around Me

Students will enjoy working with families to come up with word problems connected to various places in their homes.

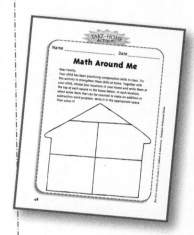

Give each child a copy of page 48 to take home. Go over the page together, reviewing the directions and letting students suggest possible problems to model the assignment. For example, students might suggest that they could label one room in the house "Kitchen," then write a word problem about cooking—for example, "If a cookie recipe calls for three eggs and there are 12 eggs in the carton, how many eggs will be left after I make the cookies?"

Word Problems From the Past

Connect history and math with word problems that take students back in time.

Model this activity by showing students an interesting historical fact that includes numbers—for example, "Clara Barton was 11 years old when she left school to care for her injured brother. She left a job at the U.S. Patent Office 30 years later in 1862 to help injured soldiers in the U.S. Civil War. How old was Clara when she became a Civil War nurse?" Invite students to write word problems using historical facts. Display the word problems on a bulletin board for classmates to solve.

Literature LINK

Fun With Numbers

by Massin (Harcourt Brace, 1993)

This picture book is full of interesting history about numbers. From why we count in sets of 60 with clocks to who used zeroes and who didn't, this book will fascinate young readers whether they are just learning to count or can add and subtract big numbers.

Name _____   Date _____

Twenty Wins

Best-Ever Activities for Grades 2–3: Addition & Subtraction Scholastic Professional Books

Name _____ Date _____

House of Addition

My Number _____

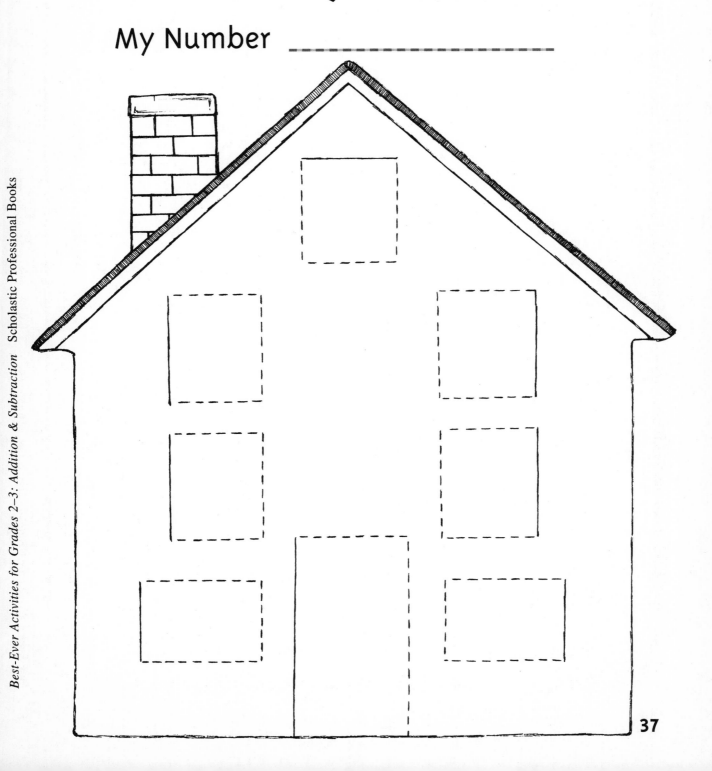

Name _____ Date _____

Math Magic

Best-Ever Activities for Grades 2–3: Addition & Subtraction Scholastic Professional Books

Name _____ Date _____

The Greatest Sum Game

Name _____ Date _____

The Greatest Sum Game

0 1 2 3 4 5 6 7 8 9

0 1 2 3 4 5 6 7 8 9

0 1 2 3 4 5 6 7 8 9

0 1 2 3 4 5 6 7 8 9

0 1 2 3 4 5 6 7 8 9

0 1 2 3 4 5 6 7 8 9

0 1 2 3 4 5 6 7 8 9

Best-Ever Activities for Grades 2–3: Addition & Subtraction   Scholastic Professional Books

Name _____   Date _____

Mail Math

Race to Zero

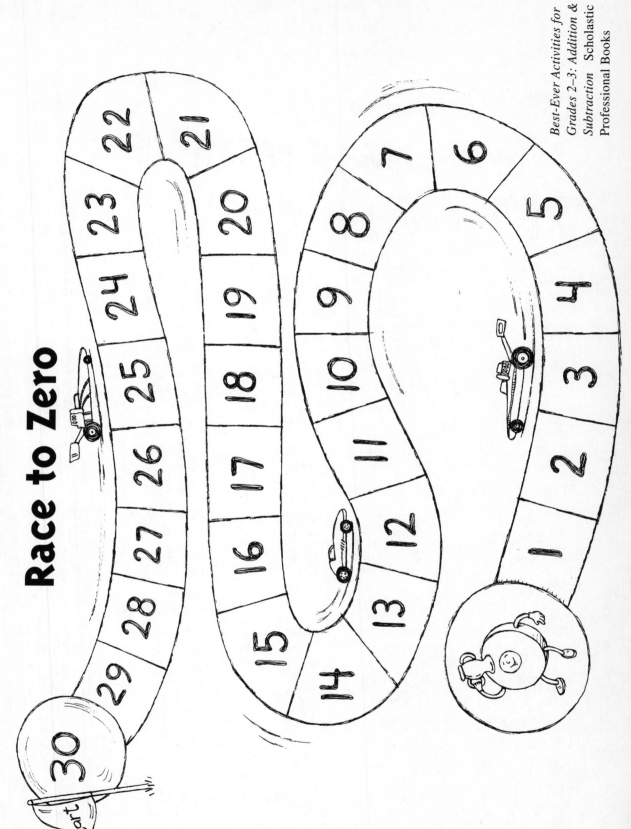

*Best-Ever Activities for
Grades 2–3: Addition &
Subtraction* Scholastic
Professional Books

Name ———————————— Date ————

Math Snack

Draw your snacks on the plate. Write an addition sentence to go with the picture!

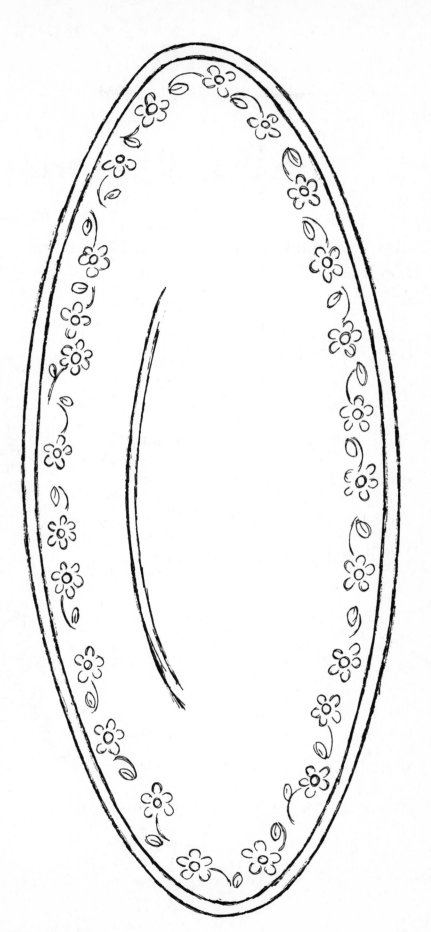

My math snack addition sentence: ————————

Best-Ever Activities for Grades 2–3: Addition & Subtraction Scholastic Professional Books

Name _____ Date _____

Subtraction Poetry

What would you like to "do subtraction" on? Complete the poem by filling in the blanks. Read your poem aloud to a friend or someone in your family. Let that person take a turn filling in the blanks to make a new poem!

Using Subtraction

I often heard the teacher say,

"Subtract means less or take away."

And so I'd get great satisfaction

If I could only do subtraction

On all of these—Yes all of these:

_____ ,

_____ ,

_____ ,

Since these all drive me to distraction,

For them I'd always use subtraction.

—Lee Blair

"Using Subtraction" by Lee Blair from ARITHMETIC IN VERSE AND RHYME (Girrard, 1971).
Best-Ever Activities for Grades 2–3: Addition & Subtraction Scholastic Professional Books

Name _____   Date _____

Make a Math Alien

Choose and write addends in the blanks. Trade papers with a partner. Complete each other's number sentences and draw the alien!

_____ + _____ = _____ eyes

_____ + _____ = _____ heads

_____ + _____ = _____ legs

_____ + _____ = _____ noses

_____ + _____ = _____ ears

_____ + _____ = _____ antennae

_____ + _____ = _____ arms

_____ + _____ = _____ hands

_____ + _____ = _____ fingers

_____ + _____ = _____ mouths

_____ + _____ = _____ bodies

Name _____   Date _____

Who Am I?

When you double me you get _____.

When you double me and add one you get _____.

I'm one less than _____.

If you add ten to me you get _____.

Who am I? _____.

Who am I?

Best-Ever Activities for Grades 2–3: Addition & Subtraction   Scholastic Professional Books

Name _____

Date _____

First off the Bridge

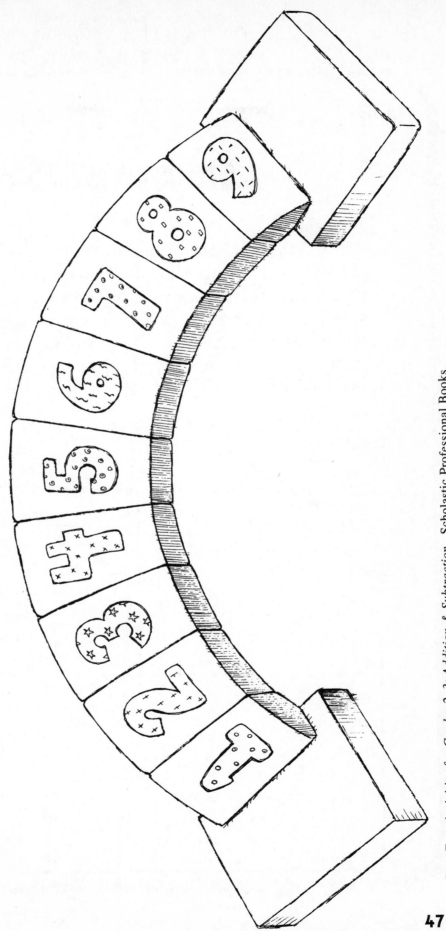

Name _____   Date _____

Math Around Me

Dear Family,
Your child has been practicing computation skills in class. Try this activity to strengthen these skills at home. Together with your child, choose four locations in your home and write them at the top of each square in the house below. In each location, select some items that can be counted to make an addition or subtraction word problem. Write it in the appropriate space. Then solve it!

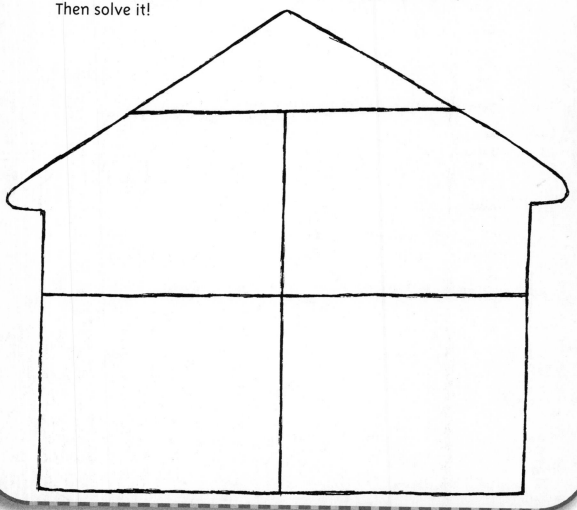

Best-Ever Activities for Grades 2–3: Addition & Subtraction Scholastic Professional Books